Journey to an idea,
Making a new difference!

By
R.O. ROURKE

TABLE OF CONTENTS

PREFACE

The whole idea behind this book is a journey of opinion. According to the Constitution of the United States is that we as a people have the right to Freedom of Speech, so here we are on a journey of sorts together, reading and thinking as to your opinions about our government.

As you read through this journey, please ask yourself questions like; Can we, do better as to our leadership at the federal, state, and local levels of government? What can we do to make a difference? And how do we define the concept of making a new difference work for us?

The last question in my opinion is the easiest to answer; Define it yourself. I can only voice my opinions as to how I would respond to this question.

Another response would be in the constitution as it says that we have the right to, "Freedom of Speech." I say use it!

So, I ask that you tag along and voice your opinions on hot topics that range from Education to opinions on Good/Bad Government and a couple of thoughts as to how we, the people can make changes.

As I close this short note of sorts, I ask for your responses, your opinions and thoughts for even though this book may be put in book form, It is my hope to keep the thoughts ever expanding!

With Respect to the People,

Robb O. Rourke

Journey to an Idea,
<u>*Acknowledgements.*</u>

Acknowledgements

Where to start? Well, this has been a very interesting project that I have under took; it's been both an adventure of fun and a learning experience.

There have been many people that I would like to thank for their thoughts and advice.

To Darryl Eaton, as a friend, I acknowledge your opinion and strong belief in the idea of being politically independent. This is something I have learned over the years of our friendship.

To Virginia Ward, "Auntie V," you are a rock. You saw leadership in me and I just want you to know that I am very greatful for your friendship and your opinions. It is still my hope to get you down here in Texas for some real good cooking!

May be you'll stay a while?

To John Reho, Jr., "Spanky," (and yes, folks he will get even with me for this. (ror) [lol]) My friend you are on a very short list of people that I could define as, "Best Friends!" You are my daughter's Godfather! Now, John please don't go Brando, on me right now, okay? We have had long discussions concerning politics, and now the basis of this book. To that I will always be greatful and in your debt.

To Mike Lane," Supreme Allied Commander," you have been straight forward with me from day one. You not only on that short list of Best Friend's, you have also been a mentor to me, and to that I am ever greatful.

You all helped in one fashion or another to the development of this book. I am greatful and truly blessed to be associated with friends like you!

Robb O. Rourke

Journey I
<u>Advocating Education</u>

In advocating Education I believe that I am just voicing an opinion. They say that it takes one voice or stone to cause a ripple effect in a pond or a community of citizens. Education has always been an interesting field to aspire to. My regret was that I did not have the discipline to expand my horizon in this field of endeavor.

I have mentioned a number of times with in this book and probably even a few more times that I worked my way through college with many different jobs, being a Substitute Teacher was just one of them. I taught many different subjects and saw many different approaches to education. Do I agree with all? No!

So, when I look to our State Legislature and the Congress in Washington as to changes in Education and see not much movement, I have to speak my mind.

The one thing I object to in politics is this idea of labeling change in an approach to an issue as Republican, opposed to being Democratic. Liberal Versus. Conservative. Topics like education, like border security, like adult literacy are issues that should be at best labeled as what's best for the Nation or much less Texas, PERIOD!

As I conclude this section, I can only say that if there is an issue that effects, in your opinion the entire community, i.e., the state and/or Country, voice your opinion. Speak your mind,

Period!

With Respect to the People,

I am

Robb O. Rourke

Journey II
A Framework of Education.

Education will be with me as I am a second generation part-time instructor (substitute teacher). My Mother taught at the local school district, and I followed her as I worked my way through college.

Education is one of a few things my former wife and I still agree on.

Education is an issue of," State's Rights," period! I just don't know of any way to put it. The Education of our Children is the responsibility of each state, not Washington!

We don't need bureaucrats, and red tape in our schools. We need educators, who will not just teach, but motivate students to learn!

We live in the information age, but that does not mean our education criteria doesn't change with the times. It means that we have a framework that is adaptable to the day!

It means that our Educators use any and all means possible that will challenge and motivate students to learn, by old fashion thinking, not by a stroke of a keypad!

It means Educators will not have red tape tying their hands limiting their ability to teach.

As to this book I will outline my thoughts and opinions that as they pertain to Education. Please note that points of reference will be designated as to Federal and State reforms.

First the Federal Reforms to ponder:

Objective: To make an effective argument that Education is:

1.) An Argument of State's Rights.
2.) The role of the (DOE) must be redefined by a cutting of Red Tape and overall government over reach.
(Note) The current President recently address this through an Executive Order, calling for a re-definition of Education in this country. And While I agree with the idea, I would like to offer a few thoughts on this subject.*
(a) A Single-framework of Education.
(b) Proper funding equally divided between Public, Charter Schools, and Voucher Programs.

While I realize that I am referencing two high ranking Republican's, I argue that issues like Education are not partisan and do not deserve such a label. Matter of fact, there are probably more issues at the State and Federal Levels that deserve action instead of labeling. Former President Ronald Reagan was of the opinion that Education was a matter of State's Rights. While I disagree with Mr. Reagan as to his wishes to close down the (DOE), I believe we can save jobs and re-define the purpose of Education in this Country.

I agree with President Trump in his efforts to reduce government over reach in Education. Simply, because like the many I think Washington does not understand the, "A, B, C's" of Education.

I believe that we need a Single-Framework or Set of Standards of Education that allow the individual states to operate and regulate Schools. This will result in limited Federal oversight.

(Note) Thoughts on oversight will be discussed later in this chapter.)*

Texas State Board of Education Candidate 2012 Barbara Cargill campaigned on the idea of a set of Standards for the Children of Texas and quite frankly, I not only agree with her, and if memory is correct I voted for her.

Standards of Education

Emphasis on grammar, phonics, handwriting, spelling and composition skills as well as a focus on serious literature in English classes.*

(Note with the ever evolving world of social media, some can construe that handwriting is a lost art. I would suggest to teach the next generation that there is a time and place for both. Ror)*

A curriculum that teaches the fundamental skills of mathematics like memorizing the multiplication and division tables and discouraging the use of calculators in elementary schools.

History curriculum standards that emphasize patriotism, the free enterprise system, our Founding Fathers, founding documents like the Constitution and the Declaration of Independence.

Health textbooks that uphold standards of Traditional Americanism.

Science Textbooks that encourage students to think, ask, and predict, have increased lab time and that presents Evolution as a theory, not as a fact!

Standards like these can be passed on to the states, who then pass on to local school districts and then to teacher's and then to students.

(Note: this framework is just an outline to build upon. This framework can be either expanded to include computers and computer technology and to educate our next generation learn and grow within the information age. ror)

The next step to look at would be testing in Education: both Achievement and teaching our students taking tests.

The first thing I would like to say on this area is in dealing with how students take tests. There have been too many reports of students saying that Achievement testing was too easy, teacher's teaching them the tests. Personally, I am of the opinion this is not teaching our children as to what they will expect in the future. We can teach them how to take tests. We can challenge them to demonstrate what they have learned!

<u>ACHIEVEMENT TESTING GUIDELINES</u>

Achievement Testing and results should be taken and processed to show true progress to every four years and not every year. Plain and simple, measuring true academic achievement can be demonstrated (grant it, in theory, ror) on a staggered schedule of every years rather than every year.

(a)   At the 4th grade level as a student nears Middle School.
(b)   At the 8th grade level as a student nears High School.
(c)   At the Senior Year of High School as a student nears graduation.

The idea is to reduce the impression of the test's being too easy and rumors of the test's being taught to the students be eliminated.

Another point to make is to teach the students how to take test. Introduce test taking in stages as each student progresses from elementary thru high school. Please note the following schedule of test as they should be introduced to students;

(a) Pre-K/Kindergarten: Introduction of Matching Tests.
(b) 1st-4th grades: Introduction of Multiple Choice, True/False, and Fill in the Blank Tests.
(c) 5th-High School: Introduction of Short Essay Exams, designed to show the expansion of knowledge of each student.

<u>*ANALYSIS:*</u>

The problem lies in the fact that there is even an issue in Education. Is Education an issue of State's Rights? I argue yes. Do we need new policy every time a new President is elected? I argue no, simply because that's the only thing consistent about the Department of Education (DOE). There is a need for a set of standards for our students to strive for. We need more Teachers in Classrooms. We do not need bureaucracy that allows even one student to drop out of school. For one student drop out is one to many!

This Framework/National Standards will allow for a new look at the idea of educating our next generations, and while this is one point or opinion, on one part of the overall topic of education, both at the federal and state levels, it is also open for continuous debate. The idea of this book is for me to provide an opinion and the debate begins, allowing continuous growth and expansion. The thing I hope to explore is a growth of an idea and a belief in how to, "Make A New Difference!"

EDUCATION REFORMS
AT
THE STATE LEVEL:

The first part dealt with reforms on the federal level; now we look at and debate state reforms.

The first step is for each state to take more responsibility as to the education of our next generation. National Standards is just a first step. The next is the up to the states. This process we could easily call, " Trickle-Down Education. "

The idea is to remove the bureaucracy that comes from a change that happens every time we elect a new President. Grant it, a new Administration brings new ideas, and a new bureaucracy meaning more, "MORE RED TAPE!" My opinions within this book do not carry a political label, they are just common sense ideas open to discussion. At the beginning of this journey I spent time trying to find where I stood politically. What found a sense of independence in thought and opinions as to where I stood politically.

Ronald Reagan argued that education was an issue of, "State's Rights." Now add to that the Libertarian opinion of, "Less government, More freedom," it could be argued that as to the idea of Education being an, " Issue of State's Rights," by removing the bureaucracy from the (DOE), re-defining it as an oversite office that

Oversees the implementation of the National Standards That I mentioned earlier.

The next step is up to the state's themselves. It could be said that all I am suggesting a shift in where the bureaucracy will be. I argue just the opposite. I am of the opinion that we as parent's, and fellow Texans are up for new ideas and challenges that will further the education of our children!

One thing to add to this discussion is putting more teachers into classrooms. The question to ask is how? My response is this; there are a lot of career oriented people that have a strong need to seek a second career for one reason or another. In other words we still a have something to contribute!

One thing I observed when I was a Substitute Teacher, as I worked my way through college, a lot of student's could have used one simple thing; to be motivated! I cite this example; I once had an assignment as a roving instructor helping students' with some extra help on problem areas. This one particular student needed help in trying to solve a simple math problem. Well, we worked and when he discovered the answer the smile on his face was all I needed.

To get back on track I suggest the idea of opening the field of teaching to those who are seeking a second career.

There are a lot of us that are looking for a second career. Either we are fulfilling a need to re-define our lives or business decisions have made it a necessity. We still have something to contribute to society, so why not teach?

I once heard that anyone could learn from a book, but where is the motivation to actually learn?

This not to say anything against teaching, it is a means to enhance the profession. Just imagine a teacher that has experience beyond a Math or English book with the ability to go that extra step and actually connect with a student that has issues learning?

I recall working with a student in an elementary school as a roving instructor, and this particular student had an issue with a simple multiplication problem; 9x7.
I helped him to solve this problem by counting the number of touchdowns (7 pts. Ror) nine times and when he discovered the answer, and well the smile on his face said enough!

Now to the idea
Of
Second-Career Teaching.

Most, if not all Universities require prospective student's to have a bachelor's degree from an accredited school. To that I agree, yet I differ in opinion. Why can't a fast track program be introduced in each School of Education at the University level?

The overall idea is to use each year of experience as a substitute (1-3 per class hours) for their area of specialization. For example a prospective student that has x number of years in a field like accounting or even politics those years would be substituted for time that would have been spent in a class room.

I realize this idea is rather simple, but look at the benefits;
(1.) More money goes to the Universities.
(2.) Jobs are created, especially for those who really want to work and still feel that they have something to contribute!

Journey III
A few more thoughts on Education

I agree with those who refer to Education as an issue of State's Rights. I agree with those who believe that Washington needs to stay away from Education, period!

Yet, I propose a few more thoughts on this particular subject.

I worked part of my undergraduate studies as a substitute teacher. My mother took pride in her tenure as a substitute teacher. And what does this have to do with anything? It just wanted to show that I and my family have had a high level of respect for our public education system, and we truly believe in it. This is not to say that a tweek here and there is not a good or bad thing. We need to remember to do the right thing!

Earlier in this Journey to an Idea, I wrote of my opinions on Education. I called on the development of a set of standards. I called for more teacher's to be put in classes. Well, there are a few more things I have to say on this subject:

In the past we have seen leaders like Governor Mitt Romney and Texas Governor George Bush voice their opinions as to Education, While I agree with some aspects of their philosophy and legislative ability to see the implementation of such. I feel there is some room to voice my thoughts of each.

Governor Romney, in a book on your thoughts and opinions you were quoted as to say," ...education has to be held at the local and state level, not at the federal level... the best thing for education is great teachers, hire the best and brightest to be teachers, pay them properly, make sure they have school choice, test them properly, make sure they are meeting the standards that need to be met, and make sure that you put the parents in charge..."

President Bush, in principle I can agree with the Testing concept of,"No Child Left Behind," I think that to show a progression a more staggered program would show a true progression of educational achievement.

Just think first, teach testing as part of the curriculum from K-12 would be an integrate aspect of the educating of our children. Second, if we staggered achievement testing to every four years as in first testing point of reference; the fourth grade, as students will soon be in Middle School; eighth grade as students are about to take that next step to High School; Senior year or twelfth grade as they are about to head to College.

In the most recent session of the Texas Legislature Senate Bill 3 (SB-3) calling for a voucher program was introduced and passed. While I am not opposed to a voucher program the idea of who is handling the transfer of funds is where I have a problem. We need to concentrate on a better plan that encompasses an adjustable framework that allows motivation, challenge and progression of the Educational system in this country. I include a recently published editorial printed in the Galveston County Daily News;

I recently read the press release from the office of State Senator Larry Taylor, Senate Bill-03 (SB3) and I felt it necessary to voice a few concerns as to this legislation.

While I could be described as, "Old School, "when it comes to Education, I am concerned as to the idea of the voucher system, and with this legislation, an inquiring mind has a question or two.

While I am of the opinion that the school board system would be the proper venue to distribute funding from the state legislature, I want to ask questions as to its implementation. The cost effectiveness and when will there be a point where the idea of using a non-profit be defined as break even?

It appears to me that funding through a new third party creates more, "Red-Tape and Bureaucracy," than before. Do we need more bureaucrats telling our schools how to and where our students can be educated, or do we find a better option?

I believe that it was Ronald Reagan that said Education was an issue of, "States' Rights," so let us see from the legislature a plan that expands the premise of Education in Texas; that includes a plan to challenge our children to think. In 2012 Candidate Barbara Cargill campaigned on the idea of a set of standards for our children to be taught. Standards; that emphasize, grammar, spelling, and a curriculum that teaches the fundamentals of math, while discouraging the use of calculators in elementary schools.

I add that this must include standards for our children to be taught how to take tests and that the so-called achievement tests be accessed every 4 years, i.e., 4th, 8th, and 12th grade. In this manner I am of the opinion students will show a true progression of an education. We need a plan to put more teachers' in our class rooms to motivate our children to learn. Some of my associates and I discussed this particular topic, especially since we have, at some level, spent some time behind a teacher's desk. The idea we came with would not only put more teachers' in class rooms, it might also reduce class sizes. A plan to educate our children must include aspects of funding of schools that includes public, charter and some form of a voucher plan based upon proportional need and reduce the amount of red-tape that ties the hands of educators in this state.

With Respect to the People of Texas,

Robb O. Rourke

p.s.

So, let me back track a bit, thanks to Former President Carter, we now have the Department of Education (DOE). I understand that with every new administration is a new agenda, but when one student slips through the cracks is that one too many. And to me this is where I have a problem. Washington does not understand as to the education process at the state level, period.

So, let's talk an idea or two:

First, it is my understanding that education funds are based upon the overall student population of each state. To that I bring back (SB-3), I am not opposed to the idea of a voucher or scholarship for low-income students. I am opposed to the implementation of this plan. A third party, whether be a non-profit, or a for profit program there has to be a better option, that does not, repeat, does not have any semblance of more red tape and bureaucracy. What Texas needs is a plan that specifically states;

(1.)   Framework of Education; a set of standards for which teachers' can actually teach.

(2.)   A program putting more teachers' in class rooms; quiet possibly reducing class size.

(3.)   A funding plan for schools that splits funds between Public, Charter and a Voucher Program.

As to point #3, I submit the following:

Funding split 3 ways as in the following manner:

Example year1 funding is split:

<u>Public Schools</u>	<u>Charter Schools</u>	<u>Voucher</u>
34%	33%	33%

In Year 3 funding would change based upon a proportional need, as in student progress and achievement, which would be followed by changes in years 5, 7, etc.

I, like most Texans believe that Education is a priority for our children, our next generation. Politics must not does not have a role in education, "PERIOD!"

The idea behind this book is to debate ideas and issues that affect each and every one.
The idea of this book was to start up a discussion, a debate on issues that affect each and every one of us.
I had such a discussion and adapted the above diagram to look like this;

<u>Public Schools</u>   <u>Voucher Programs</u>
75%   25%

Funding will be adapted in a similar format like that of above simply because the Texas legislature meets every two years.

Another option I have worked with before would be to take a percentage off the top from every department under the state budget. With this option extra money can be allocated for Education Funding.

With respect to the People,

Robb O. Rourke

Journey IV

<u>*Adult Literacy*</u>

While I am not an expert on this topic, I can say that I have experienced both ends of the spectrum on this.

The former Mrs. Rourke, well what can one say about an ex and not get a laugh or two, but that's not the point of this part of this book. I have also experienced an association with a young lady that spent some time homeless, but had a unique quality, she taught herself how to read and write via the use of a smart phone. While this could be a line and I am the most gullible person in the world I have witnessed her writings via, text messages and her general conversation, and my best guess that her education is a very slow process, but it's working, for I have seen general progress in writings and overall conversation ability.

I also realized that Literacy problems in general are an issue that we should of concern. At the beginning of this piece I stated that I am not an expert on this topic, but I wanted to voice my opinion as to something that may be helpful?

The idea is to connect People in Adult Literacy Programs with smartphones and air/data time, of course with literacy applications (APPS) already frontloaded on their phones.

The problem lies in getting the suppliers, i.e., Cellphone companies to agree.

So, I propose the following;

That for every Cellphone company that participates, i.e. , in donating phones and provide a sliding scale to make payment, as in air time/data to Adult Literacy Programs they will receive tax credits or breaks from the State of Texas.

The idea is to connect people with technology. Connect people with the ability to adapt to an ever changing world and actually learn from it this can be a win-win scenario for all sides:

Cellphone companies will receive tax credits or breaks from the State. Participants in these literacy programs would receive access to not just a phone, but a means to further themselves in life.

What can be done to correct this issue? In my opinion this is just one thought, but it is a thought that has what I believe to be a lot of potential to be something that work and give support the common everyday person.

I have always believed in the good of every American. And I believe in the idea of helping where I can I mentioned my former wife. There are a few things that we agreed upon Education is one and giving back to the community is the other.

We supported many a different cause and to some extent I want to say that we, both still do.

Adult Literacy I have encountered some that have succeeded and demonstrated their abilities to comprehend events in front of them. I have also encountered those who have knowledge, but don't know how to communicate. I have also experienced one who has made the attempt to broaden her view of the world and I wish her well!

Journey V
<u>*Advocating Ideas*</u>

The idea of these few pages is to remind us, the people of this great country, that we have a voice that wants to be heard. Our Constitution clearly states that we have the right to voice our opinions, "Freedom of Speech."

Our history has demonstrated that we have, through many examples, believed in one ideal,

"FREEDOM!

So, over this chapter and maybe a few others, we can talk about freedom and how one can advocate for those ideas that will continue to make us free.

In advocating education I believe that I am just voicing an opinion. They say that it takes one voice or stone to cause a ripple effect in a pond or a community of citizens. Education has always been an interesting field to aspire to. My regret was that I did not have the discipline to expand my horizon in this field of endeavor.

I have mentioned a number of times with in this book and probably even a few more times that I worked my way through college with many different jobs, being a Substitute Teacher was just one of them. I taught many different subjects and saw many different approaches to education. Do I agree with all? No!

As to immigration, I think a majority of Americans can agree on Border Security and immigration, but a Wall?

So, when I look to our State Legislature and the Congress in Washington as to changes in Education and see not much movement, I have to speak my mind.

The one thing I object to in politics is this idea of labeling change in an approach to an issue as Republican, opposed to being Democratic. Liberal Versus. Conservative. Topics like education, like border security, like adult literacy are issues that should be at best labeled as what's best for the Nation or much less Texas, PERIOD!

As I conclude this section, I can only say that if there is an issue that effects, in your opinion the entire community, i.e., the state and/or Country, voice your opinion. Speak your mind,

Period!

On another of this chapter is advocating for Good, not Bad Government.

John F. Kennedy said, "...ask not what your country can do for you. Ask what you can do for your country."

To me this means sending a message to our leaders when we want change. A great example is that of the battle over health care. I have always been of the opinion that some issues do not need a partisan label, when it is an issue of the people. Health Care could fall under this category. Education is another.

When The Affordable Care Act, ie, (Obama Care) first came up for a vote national polls indicated that the public was against it. Yet, congress voted for it and the President signed it into law.

Today, Obama Care is about to be repealed simply due to a Republican decision. Do I feel this is wrong? YES! What we need is a law that makes insurance accessible, and affordable to a public that will be cut from those who actually have insurance they purchased without the help of (Obama Care).

Again we need to send our message to Washington and let our Leaders that we are tired of the lack of progress in the name of partisanship and work for the people.

As I conclude this section, I can only say that if there is an issue that effects, in your opinion the entire community, i.e., the state and/or Country, voice your opinion. Speak your mind,

Period!

With Respect to the People,

Robb O. Rourke

Journey VI

Advocating Ideas on Immigration

The President wants a wall along our southern border with the Country of Mexico, and while I can agree something needs to be done, I question the rationale behind the Presidents' opinion.

The Federal Government controls our borders, but yet does Washington, and the President understand what goes on near the southern border with Mexico? And if I remember correctly Texas Law and border security patrol beyond that.

Will this wall stop the flow of illegal contraband crossing our border, I don't think so, and have to ask the President if he remembers an escape felon from a high, repeat, high security prison, who tunneled out of the facility and now in solitary in a U.S. Prison? What can be done? Maybe, a Texas solution!

Try this for size; Let me start off on a sidebar bit of information, I'm a bit of a history buff, so this will play into this train of thought.

In his memoirs, "Decision Points," Former President wrote of his discussions with then Mexican President Vincente Fox, as to the subject of immigration. It looked as if both leaders approached this topic from very different directions. President Bush wrote of the positives of a guest worker program and President Fox likened the idea of, "regularization."

The idea of regularization had its pitfalls, which were automatic citizenship once some arrives in this country. At the time of 9/11 this proposal could also mean a very open border for would be terrorists to exploit.

During his campaign for President, Mitt Romney was quoted to say at a GOP debate in 2011, "...we are a nation of immigrants. We love legal immigration.

But for legal immigration to work, we need to secure the border and we also have to crack down on employers that hire people are here illegally."

While these were opinions, let me suggest an idea or two to ponder.

Journey VII
<u>Differences in Culture</u>

A few thoughts on Differences of Culture?

I watched the Fox Channel (KRIV-TV/Ch.26) the other night and heard a very open and opinionated discussion over Sanctuary Cities. And while I may agree with some finer points made in the discussion, I also had a few concerns.

Yes, we are, "A Nation of Immigrants," but does that entitle us to display a bias simply because they are a people of a Different Culture? I would like to say No, to that, "How about you?"

To that I add a few thoughts and opinions. Illegal Immigration along the Southern Border will always be a hot-topic issue, period, but how do we separate those who want to come to America versus those who are escaping to America?

The President wants to build a wall, along our southern border. Build it and they shall not come?

President Trump can you say, "El Chapa?"

Well, as a student of History, here are a few thoughts of mine to ponder:

After the end of World War II, President Truman with the aid of General George C. Marshall, formulated, and processed through the legislative system a plan to rebuild Western Europe and prevent the spread of Communism. This was the Marshall Plan.

I propose, via your opinions, something a bit similar for Texas. So, instead of arguing as to who belongs and legalities as to who do not belong, why doesn't the state shift its concerns to supporting the infrastructure of the of the states, i.e., Small business' that have a Latino employees, by giving them tax cuts and/or breaks in an effort to encourage said employees to enroll, attend and pass citizenship classes.

Let me expand on this thought;

1.) *We do not need to see similar events to happen here as they did in Arizona this past February (2017). Granted she did violate immigration law, I suggest this idea is and will not be used as a means to gather information on Latino's', who have resettled in Texas. This idea or proposal is meant to not just help them with an alternative means, i.e., becoming citizens of the United States, not to live in fear as to what may happen if and when that, so-called knock on the door from immigration comes.*

2.) *This idea will help Small businesses with tax breaks/cuts as they encourage their employees to enroll, attend and pass these citizenship classes.*

3.) *The tax breaks/ cuts can be defined as primary and secondary;*

(a) *Primary tax breaks/cuts; will be defined based upon the number of employees and family members sign up, attend and pass these classes.*

(b) *Secondary tax breaks/cuts; will be defined based on the number of employees that need to be sponsored.*

4.) *Eligibility;*

To be eligible a small business must have Latino employees as part of their overall staff. Said employees must be employed a minimum of 1-3 years for the small business to eligible for tax breaks.

With Respect to the People of Texas,

Robb O. Rourke

Journey VIII
Good/Bad Government

Good Government/Bad Government

Open Letter to Speaker Paul Ryan;

Dear Sir;

I write this letter to ask a simple question, "How do we propose to restore and maintain the American Dream... (1) At Home and (2) Abroad?"

I can easily quote Former President Clinton and his ideas from his book, " Back to Work," but decided to only use that tactic as a last resort and just talk one on one.

Like the majority of Americans, I am on twitter. I don't read many of the tweets as others do, simply because I don't have the time! But, I read a tweet from Senator J. Thune, as to Trump Care being the Republican Fixit for the very ailing Obama Care. Sir, my biggest gripe with government in the partisan divide. Nothing gets done unless its' done by the party in charge. Yes, I am a Democrat and frankly, I have a few choice words for them as well! Health Care is a very hot topic issue in this country and we need a solution that works, period!

We have issues in this country, both on the Federal and State levels. Here in Texas we have our share of issues from Education, Border Control, and even an issues as to rest rooms.

I have voiced my thoughts to issues like education and the environment of Galveston Bay, and the lack of effort from Leadership at both the state and federal levels to work together on a bipartisan solution.

As to the President's Wall along the southern border with Mexico, great political fodder, but getting the Government of Mexico to pay for it, "Right?"

We need answers that will make America great, again! Not politics as usual!

As to Health Care, let's get the facts straight, polls indicate when Obama Care first came up for a vote the American People did not agree with Congress. Yet, it passed. Instead of repealing the Affordable Care Act, why didn't legislators just try to make changes that would get approval from the American People?

The most recent issue of the USA Today had a headline that indicate Congress' popularity at 12%. I'm sorry, but that's nothing to brag about. You tweeted that the Congress is working together in a positive manner seems just the exact opposite of this headline. Mr. Ryan, we need leadership from Washington, what we are getting sounds a lot like the same old garbage.

Why can't the Republican leadership simply ask the Democrats to help save Health Care?

Sir, I was taught that our government was a, "...Government of the People, by the People and for the People." I still believe that and I am willing to believe that the majority of Americans still do!

Speaker Ryan you are a member of the House Leadership and frankly someone, a Democrat could respect. Please Sir, lead!

Speaker Ryan, Former President Reagan called Washington a shining light on the hill, we as a people need to believe in that once again!

This chapter will deal with my opinions and thoughts on Good/ Bad Government.

A former co-worker said that if he was President, he would govern this country on tough love! To sum up the responses as to this train of thought can be summed up in one word, "HOW?" And with that asked, one can understand the fact that no rational response came about. To me the difference between Good and Bad Government is doing the job. Making the right decisions that will lead our country to a better tomorrow. (yes, I know that sounds like a political line, still it makes a point as to a difference of opinion, ror)

Former President Clinton in his book, "Back to Work," wrote

...America at its core is an idea—the idea that no matter who you are or where you're from, if you work hard and play by the rules, you'll have freedom and opportunity to pursue your dreams and leave your kids a country where they can chase theirs... Work is about more than making a living...It's fundamental to human dignity, to our sense of self-worth as useful, independent, free people...

To that statement I can only agree!

As a government that statement is something to govern by. It has no party labels. It has no labels of political opinion, period!

We as a nation have many problems and challenges, at both the federal and state levels of government, that need to find common ground that will lead to the correct solution.

President Clinton wrote, "I believe the challenges we face, which are tough enough on their own, are made even more difficult by the highly polarized, deeply ideological political climate in Washington." (2011. p.11)

My question can anyone disagree? Frankly, there would be a small majority that agree with this statement.

Today, the biggest hot topic issue, other than the latest POTUS tweet, is Health Care.

While I agree with the intent of the Affordable Care Act, I am more amazed at the fact that the people we elected to govern ignored the fact that polls indicated that the majority of America did not like it! Yet, we now have what history will call, "Obama Care."

After hearing several years of Republican groans of repealing this particular piece of legislation, we now have, "Trump Care," and a POTUS that acts like if he doesn't get his way he'll let Obama Care die a slow death.

So, Let us go back to my former co-worker and ask how would his tough love agenda come up with an answer to this problem? We're waiting!

The answer does not lie in coming up with a Republican fixit solution for a Democratic problem.

The answer lies in trying to find common ground, a framework that could be expanded to make this issue work and give our citizens access to proper health care.

My biggest grip with government deals with Education. I agree with POTUS and his directives to find a means of reducing government overreach into education. It was once said that Former President Reagan was of the opinion that Education was an issue of State's Rights.

Education is an issue of State's Rights, Period! Washington needs to limit or totally remove themselves from the idea of educating our children. While I think rather highly of Former President Carter, I must disagree with him on Education. While the idea of a Department of Education, (DOE), made sense the fact that education agendas changed with every new administration elected to govern, I disagree because in theory it would allow for students to fall through the cracks of the new agenda at hand. What we as a country need a system of Education that allows of limited government oversight and more state level involvement.

Former President George W. Bush's, "No Child Left Behind," had its merits as in the idea of testing the progress of our children in school. My biggest fear were not just the children that fell cracks, some of the ideas associated with it. While I am not in disagreement with the idea of a voucher

program for low income families. I think we could do better. (Please note the chapter on education)

I believe in a plan that would involve both the Federal and State Governments.

Please excuse me for borrowing from the Reagan Years,

Trickledown Education.

Trickledown Education simply allows the State levels of government to adapt and implement education policy within a framework of standards. To put more teachers in the classrooms and reducing the overall size. To introduce how to take tests as a student progresses through K-12 grade levels. To continue the idea of achievement testing, not every year, but staggered to every four years. Example; Fourth Grade, then 8th, and then 12th. This formula, in theory should show a progression of learning from K-12.

As far as funding of Education from Federal to State, the current formulas should stay in place. As to a Voucher program, like I noted a page or two ago that I am not in disagreement with the idea. Despite my differences over Texas Senate Bill-3 calling for a Voucher Program to be run by a third party, a non-profit organization, I take issue. This plans smells like a dead fish. It is just wrong. We all, I hope agree that dealing with red tape and possibly more red tape is not the way to educate our children. I would propose a different plan that would balance funding between Public Charter Schools and a Voucher Program.

To get back to the idea of Good/Bad Government, to simply put it we need a government that is willing to work together and not, repeat not show their partisan colors!

Our Founding Father's referred to our Government as

"... A Government of the People, By the People and For the People!"

Journey ooIX

EYES ONLY!

For Your Eyes Only, a title of a Popular Spy novel and movie; with a meaning clouded in secret.

Eyes Only in the Intelligence World means TOP SECRET! In the Intelligence Community of every civilized nation this phrase means a lot.

In this chapter I will voice my opinions as to our Intelligence Community, (Intel). As a History buff my area of interest has been Post WWII, aka the Cold War era of our history.

In my reading I discovered many tales of a very different area of intelligence that could not be found in the Assignments of James Bond.

There is one bit of trivia that might be just considered, the influence of 007 were originally assigned to the Master Spy by his Spy Master, Ian Fleming. He served in British Intelligence and met many of the original founding operatives of what is now our modern spy agencies. Matter of fact there was a reference in a Bond novel, For Special Services, as to Mr. Fleming's input to the National Security Act of 1947, and the development of the Central Intelligence Agency, (CIA).

To my understanding the objective of our Intelligence Community is to;

Gather Intelligence, access, advise, and respond.

As to the history of our Intelligence Community, the National Security Act of 1947 was a response to Soviet infiltration of Western Intelligence at the end of WWII.

As a results of the Tragedy of 9/11 we have some new members of the Intelligence Community; the Department of Homeland Security and a Director of National Intelligence.

Today, we have a potus that a rather dim view of our Intelligence Community. I respond by saying that maybe we need to redefine our Intelligence Community Leadership into something similar to that of the National Security Council, (NSC). This is an idea that I have been pondering since 9/11. If we redefine this committee along the lines of the (NSC), we might be better organized, as to a means of reacting to situations as they present themselves.

I believe this Committee would involve every member of our Intelligence Community from the CIA, Federal Bureau Investigation, (FBI), National Security Agency, (NSA), and various military intelligence agencies. This Committee would be co-chaired by the Director of National Intelligence and the Vice President. The objective would then be access and advise the President.

44.

<u>***ANALYSIS;***</u>

Despite a dim view on the Intelligence Community, I say to the President, "Sir, this is our first line of Defense against a Foreign Threat. We not only need the capability of boots on the ground, we need eyes on the ground to lead our troops into any response that can be defined as a threat to our security, Period!

On a personal note we as a nation must remember who laid the ground work that our," First Defenders," have a means to keep our borders secure for hostile threats.

(*Author's note: I've seen too many of these movies, lol, ROR)

Journey X

Advocating for Jobs and the Economy

<u>Jobs</u>

Like a couple of Chapters earlier, I made a few suggestions as to topics that I voiced opinions on; Jobs and the Economy.

Jobs, while I looked at this from a specific perspective; making more teacher's available to teach. I realize that there are a number of programs trying to do the same, I am of the perspective that we can do better.

And doing better is defined by utilizing those who have been shown the door, simply because they can't keep up with change. There are probably a rather large portion of the population still feel as if they have something to contribute. So, the second career as a teacher. Let those candidates go back to college and be fast tracked, using their, on the job experience, as a basis for what they will be teaching.

Anyone can teach from a book. So why not let someone with outside experience motivate beyond said book.

The Economy

The national unemployment rate according to reports is around 4.5%. In Texas a bit better, estimated at 4.6%. Our objective as a people and our leadership in Austin and much less Washington need to do better by not advocating the idea of making a new difference. That idea is to work together, simply because it will remind us and rest of the world that we as a nation agree, "...that we will 'NEVER' fade into the background."

Our forefathers believed in a dream, and that led to Nation and a belief in an ideal!

Our goal is to keep that ideal alive, which means going the extra mile and without any doubts making sure that everyone can afford to, "... have a chicken in every pot."

This past June I submitted for publication an open letter to State Senator Larry Thompson (R-11) from Texas asking why funding for Galveston Bay to test for toxins has not happened for the past four years. Side note, while I understand that a study hear and one there may not show significant results, but when the state stops funding for testing I have to voice my opinions and thoughts.

Open letter to Larry Taylor

Larry Taylor:

I have a concern and wanted, like many of us that live within your Senate District, your thoughts and opinions as to a cause of actions in response to the discussion on the fact that seafood has not been tested for toxins over the past four years.

According to a new public service program on Fox Channel 26 airing this past May 02, 2017 had an interesting, yet brief discussion as to the fact that the Texas Commission on Environmental Quality, (TECQ) has not, repeat has not tested the seafood supply, i.e., fish, etc. for toxins. As a B.O.I., from Galveston I am a bit concerned as to the fact that nothing has been done for four years as to the testing of seafood in our bay?

In understanding the economy, my research looked back to the simple ideas that made this country a great nation; putting people to work and support for the small business man.

In this chapter I wrote my thoughts as to what I have done and will continue to advocate on. I believe in seeing people earn their livelihood. Supporting their families!

Earlier in this book I wrote about job growth as part of my opinions on education reform. To simply put it, in theory Universities would benefit by the increase in tuitions per semester. The State would benefit for teacher's being certified, more regulatory fees being paid. Schools would benefit simply for the fact that more teachers would be hired, and our children would benefit, simply for the fact that they would actually learn.

Now to a negative: at the bottom of page 64, I copy and pasted a couple of paragraphs from an open letter to State Senator Larry Taylor. My concerns on this matter are not just on the environment, I am concerned about the Economy of Galveston Bay,

Larry, please do not respond by issuing a political statement, in other words we do not need a response saying it's conservative vs. liberal or Republican vs. Democrat. What we need is a straight answer as to why the (TECQ) has not tested seafood in Galveston Bay over the past four years.

I grew up on Galveston Island, matter of fact proud it. There has always been two things that Galveston has always been famous for;

(1.) Tourism.
(2.) Seafood.

Tourism will always create jobs for the island, but seafood that's a different kettle of fish, (sorry. Ror)

Over the years Galveston has been a hub for Good Seafood, period. The seafood industry, my guess is somewhere around 50% of the Economy of Galveston.

To stop funding for testing of toxins does not make any bit of sense.

In doing some research, I googled studies on Cancer rates in our area from seafood and I am glad to see that research has been done by many different organizations. Yet, my question still stands, Larry, why hasn't the (TECQ) been testing seafood samples from Galveston Bay for the past four years? In the discussion, last night there was a brief, but yet informative reference to a dollar figure to renew the testing of seafood from Galveston Bay totaling $300,000.00 dollars and "the Rainy Day Fund."

And yes it was asked and quickly brushed aside as to why can't we tap into," the Rainy Day Fund," and pay for testing of the seafood from Galveston Bay? While that the rainy fund is to be used for emergency status only, doesn't the fact that testing has not happened for four years, possibly compromising the economy of your district?

Here's a thought, why not introduce legislation asking for .5 to 1% of the rainy day fund, every two years as the legislature is in session to go to the testing of seafood in Galveston Bay?

The idea of this chapter was to advocate for jobs and the economy. As I write I am advocating for a way to make a new difference in Texas. My advice is to find an issue that catches your attention and voice your opinion, whether it be a conversation with a friend around the corner to a letter to the editor, much less a book on your thoughts and concerns, always continue to advocate. To voice your opinions!

With Respect to the People,

Robb Rourke

Journey XI
Foreign Policy: National Security.

I believe that this particular can best be summed up by paraphsing the Words of John F. Kennedy; we drink the same water. We breathe the same air and we share this small planet!

And I might add one other thought; we as American's believe in and defend one idea, "FREEDOM!"

With events changing around the world quicker than what could best be described as the time of day changing from Sunday to Monday. Knowledge of foreign ideologies should be defined as a must as our world keeps changing. Gone are the Days of calling someone a communist. Our world can look at that point of reference as part of History, "The Cold War!"

The Cold War was a serious point of history as the world changed from that of a peaceful culture to a culture of rebuilding from a war.

There were steps taken with both positive and negative results.

We as a society have also seen the good, the bad and the very ugly of this era in history.

Today, we look to the present with a hope and trust in our government to make sure that our world is heading in the right direction.

To this topic I voice my thoughts and opinions;

First, we should totally support our allies and associations with groups like NATO, period. I must also add this one caveat that I agree with potus as to other members, pay their fair share.

I believe in the United Nations, and the idea, not leading to a one government world, as a united front against freedom is the right organization to correct any global conflicts.

Today we, see via the news media conflicts in multiple areas. North Korea appears to be the lead story and our pending response.

Well, our response must be decisive and complete, for the simple fact that we, as the United States will support our allies, aka, The Republic of South Korea.

The big question is how do we get there? I would say to look to our intelligence community, this apparatus must be considered a first line of defense against potential aggression against an American interest.

We must then look to other player in the region for support, i.e., gathering intelligence and opinions for analysis as we decide on our plan of action. In this instance China and Russia.

In the more recent past we have seen limited help from the government in Beijing. We need their assistance in scenario as a means of a back channel to the North Korean government. We need to persuade assistance in swaying Ponyang that a nuclear North Korea does not make a friendly North Korea, ready to be a member of the global community.

Russia, is a completely different kettle of fish. Vladimir Putin, the President of All of Russia.

What seems to me that in dealing with Putin, our leaders seem to ignore the fact that he, at one time was the head of Russian Intelligence, the KGB. The man could best be described as a self-proclaimed power leader of Russia.

We need a separate plan to act and respond to a country, a culture and a leader, who believes in a more up to date system comparable to, "Mother Russia," of the Cold War!

In my opinion the real deal as to how to react to the Putin Factor is to respect that he is the leader of Russia. We also need to look back at the history, via media reports of the man since he became President. Analysis; He is not James Bond!

Frankly, it is my hope that potus gives Putin a reason to support our responses simply for the fact that Ponyang could easily redirect their missiles toward Moscow!

As to our options;

Please note that while I have yet to be in this position as President, I understand the ramifications of actions taken.

<u>OPTIONS OF RESPONSE;</u>

Look to other players in the region for support, as in a back Channel to the opposition.

Economic responses, as in dealing with North Korea must be specific and direct. This is a country that is isolated, and wants attention. A nuclear missile that could reach the United States.

Wrong!

My analysis of the North Korean Government can very easily be defined as that of the spoiled angry child having a fit!

It says a lot about the culture of a nation, so isolated from the rest of the world, feel it necessary to bring it to the brink of War?

The next option: Military Response.

Please note that while I have three former Stepsons, two of which served in Iraq and Afghanistan, I have the utmost respect for the job they did and will continue to respect all three if they served in any action in service of freedom.

I believe that while I yet to be elected, the biggest challenge to me would be committing lives to being in harm's way, period!

I believe that our response as government, as a nation needs to be as one! We can look back to history and the period that covered, "The Cold War Era." We can learn from both steps forward and missteps taken in the name of Freedom!

Added thoughts/ Summary Analysis

In defining Foreign policy we need to look at all aspects from National Security and Global Allies to International Trade to Foreign Aid.

As to our standing in the Global picture, we have problems around the world.

As to developing a workable strategy in dealing with North Korea; the simplest response would be to define the leadership as a spoiled angry child.

The reality is that leadership of North Korea is bent on the idea of correcting a perceived wrong by attacking the source of their problem, the United States of America.

U. S. Intelligence has indicated that Russia made an attempt to disrupt our Elections in 2016.

Recently, potus made an overture to Russian Leadership as to a Joint Task on Cyber Security?

The idea of an Intelligence Community is two-fold;

1.)   Gather, Access, and react to any source that is deemed a threat to our security.
2.)   Spread miss-information.

History has shown that U.S. Policy toward Russia could easily be defined as, "...at arms- length!"

Past history has indicated Russian meddling in Western Efforts.

And today, news reports have indicated a joint venture between Russia and the United States to fight Cyber Security.

Intelligence found evidence that the Election of 2016 was a cyber attempt to influence the election.

The security of this country and our allies is a priority, period!

The leadership of this country must support the idea!

And while I agree with potus that organizations like the North Atlantic Treaty Organization, (N.A.T.O.) that a balance in funding between members must be a priority done in a timely manner.

The United Nations, (U.N.) was envisioned by Franklin D. Roosevelt as a neutral place where Global Conflicts can be averted.

To maintain specific direction to foreign policy these organizations must be a recognized point of reference in dealing with global conflicts in support of," Freedom."

The next chapter will take a brief look at Foreign Trade, and Foreign Aid.

Journey XII
TERRORISM

Terrorism can be defined in many differing context, yet the easiest definition is probably the best:

"People kill other people in the name of a cause."

History has given the world many examples of Terrorism and terrorist;

Carlos, the Jackal, a.k.a., Ilyich Ramirez Sanchez, "The World's Most Dangerous Man," was linked to many of the most horrific terrorist incidents during the Cold War Era, from the kidnapping of (OPEC), Oil Producing Economic Countries; the kidnapping and murder of members of the Israeli National Olympic Team in Munich, (West) Germany in 1972; to the events to led to the Israeli Military response in Entebbe, Uganda in 1976.

Today, Carlos spends in time in Prison serving a life term!

9/11.

Osama bin Laden.

Al-Qaeda!

Shook the very foundation we as a country believed in. The United States attacked! This was the first incident since Pearl Harbor sending us into WWII.

During the Cold War, the policy of this country was to respond to a specific threat to National Interests.

That threat was usually defined with a Soviet connection. Terrorism was a subject of a different flavor. Terrorist, while fighting based upon a cause has accepted advice from questionable sources that were against Western, or American opinions.

Today, Isis, or Isisl, is a different subject kettle of fish. They're objective it appears is to use Social Media and spread their doctrine of hate. And if you object, your, "DEAD!"

The policy of this Nation and many other is to not negotiate with terrorist, period!

The mistake in this policy is when we misjudge those who are peaceful for those who are not!

We have many citizens of the Muslim faith living in this Country, and while I don't accept the argument as to stereotyping a person simply because of their religion and nationality, My suggestion to our citizens to look back during the Cold War and see the lives scarred and ruined simply because they were called, "Communist!"

I believe that we as in our Leadership, in Washington, needs to tweek our course of response to scenarios that are defined as a threat to National Interests with a clear and specific response. Washington also must look to the citizenship and work to see a national response and not one based upon something other than facts.

We as a nation, must be treated as one, united simply because we share a single belief in freedom and we are not judged based upon the color of our skin and nationality.

To Terrorism, we as a country have a special belief in Freedom. While you may not agree with my way of life, Don't Be the One to Fire the First Shot!

I am an American!

Journey XIII
<u>Foreign Trade and Foreign Aid.</u>

Well, I must admit that the topics of this chapter are not my area of expertise, yet I am attempting to try. Wish me luck?

(ror)

As to the civics classes that I spent time in the main thing I learned in dealing with Foreign trade was that your product, i.e., American products would be sold abroad and new markets would open to American products. Foreign products would then be introduced to American Markets. In theory, this would develop into a system that would create a better global economy.

In my opinion the explanation or example would be that of the principle of B.F. Skinner's Stimulus Response Psychology

(S-R) or Operant Conditioning.

We as a country are willing to Trade x number of metric tons of rice to China and/or Japan for their markets to be sold in exchange allowing products like Toyota vehicles to be sold in America.

The big issue is when the trade becomes tilted in favor of those we have been trading with, resulting an imbalance in the market.

We should then respond with implementing tariffs or Taxes placed upon the Products that are trying to enter our ports.

I conclude this section by saying that we as a country need to look at foreign trade as a means to keep markets open and the global economy equally growing.

Foreign Aid

Well, as this section starts the best that I can say that revising will occur as soon as possible, for the simple reason there is more to say on this topic.

Foreign Aid is defined as helping under developed nations a chance to stand on their own. Global projects from supporting Aids in Africa to Human Trafficking in Mexico.

Foreign Aid is not defined as getting Mexico to pay for a wall built along our Southern Border.

Our government budgets funds for assistance to countries, as a means for the United States to demonstrate the ideas of Democratic ways.

My problem lies in knowing the answer to this question, "What happens to funding when funding goes awry?"

The point I want to make is that if we send funds to Specific countries in Africa for the Treatment of HIV and Aids, I want to make sure that it gets there.

I believe that the Federal government needs a level of control as to an accounting of monies spent on projects at hand. The thing is that I and many of the readers of this little venture, have kind hearts, but when it comes to our government using our tax dollars for something other than what it was designated for, might have a differing opinion or two!

Journey XVI
<u>*Social Security*</u>

Social Security, a product of the New Deal and Franklin D. Roosevelt, was designed to give support seniors as an aid in their retirement. Social Security has gone through many battles to keep afloat since FDR.

As to its history Social Security is a legacy to be revered and respected for what it stands for, period!

As a student of American history, I would argue that in respect to memory of a great, if not the greatest leader of the 20th Century, is an objective worthy of a continuous fight, simply because at that time this country was at its lowest moment and it took a man in a wheelchair to show us, as a nation to get up and once again stand tall.

In the election of 2016 I watched, like most of us with great interest as to the outcome this past November.

I was glad to see that one of the candidates for President, Senator Bernie Sanders had an idea concerning the future of Social Security.

Briefly, Senator Sanders plan makes sense as a means of securing the future of this great program. Like everyone who earns a check, has monies deducted, withholding, social security, etc. While the deductions vary, as does income across America, the idea of everyone having the same percentage deducted for social security makes sense, for this reason going back to each individual pay check if everyone had the same percent deducted for social security, the government would then see a larger input into an aging system as a means of securing it for generations to come.

And while I must admit that I did not vote for the Senator, I did support my party in the election working on voter registration for the election, that came and went as the candidate of the party did not win.

America means freedom. America means belief in oneself.

America has had many examples of leadership and lofty goals that were challenges to us all to do better, in life overall.

One can remember the words of Franklin D. Roosevelt in 1933, "The only thing we have to fear is fear itself..."

And what of the challenge of John F. Kennedy, "Ask not what your Country can do for you. Ask what you can do for your Country?" Did we as a nation see the challenge of the future?

Did we not once again, stand tall and show the world a belief that could lead the world?

To that I respond, it's time to,

"Make a New Difference!"

Journey XVIII
Equal Parental Rights

It was once theorized that it took a community to raise a family. In the right context this theory is possibly right as if one defines a family as that community. And the purpose of this journey is to explore my journey a topic of my actions over the years.

I divorced my former wife over ten years ago, leaving behind Daddy's Little Character, my daughter in the care of her Mother. I like many men in this scenario can say that I am a Divorced Dad.

Research over the years has led me to some unique discoveries;

1.)   The parameters of the family court system were outdated and appeared to be a bit bias toward the non-custodial parent.

2.)   The idea of the best interest of the child has seen a way from the idea of best interest to that of can put up the best argument to the court.

3.)   My observations over the years seen a movement away from the idea of what can be defined as in the best interest of the child.

I could argue that my rights were trampled upon by the family court system. I can honestly state that I never received a notice of a hearing docking a specific amount from my paycheck every week, for Child Support. This is not to say that I would have objected, I was and still am of the opinion that it was the best option at the time for me to support my daughter.

I could easily argue as to every word I said in front of the legal system and bureaucrats. But, I will not simply because I came to realize this was not a war or battle between the former Mrs. Rourke and I, what mattered was what was in the best interests of our daughter, who I love and respect every day of her life. My objective then became a

Mission of seeking the equal responsibility of both parents despite the family was wrecked by divorce.

I once campaigned for Congress with part of my platform dedicated to seeing that equal parental responsibility continued after a divorce.

Today, I look at Texas and see a bit of change in this area of concern. A couple of years ago I gave testimony to a legislative committee concerned with legislation call for an Equal Parental Rights Act. That act must truly define an equal balance of responsibility of commitment of parent, even after a divorce.

And while I am glad that Governor Abbott introduced an executive order calling for more state control as to a balance of responsibility by both parents when it comes to what's in the best interests of the child. I must express concerns as to if it will be able to stand up to a legal challenge from the courts. I do recall a similar piece of legislation on the federal level as to non-custodial parent, i.e., usually the father is placed in jail for non-payment of child support.

This I believe was challenged and defined as unconstitutional as it would put the father in a position of not being able to earn money and support our children.

At the beginning I mentioned that it took a community to raise a family. If one defines that community as the perspective makes a bit of sense. The problem still lies in the fact that once a divorce occurs a father must fight a painful uphill battle to insure the support needed for the children.

Journey XIX
Politics as Usual?

While I have a level respect for James Carville, I must disagree with the tactics of strictly blaming Donald Trump. Frankly, a challenge and debate of his policies makes more sense. While I am a Democrat by nature, even though I have spent time in republican and libertarian camps, I will always believe in the idea of a government of the people...

We as Democrats, across must stop mud- slinging, partisan politics of Washington and talk about finding common ground as to ideas to make a difference, America.

We have seen eight years of partisan politics under the previous administration. We have seen polls indicating policies opinions the people said no too. We have seen polls indicating all- time lows for congress, in the eyes of the people.

We as a people voted in Donald Trump as President. While, I can disagree with POTUS, it's not because he's republican, to simply put it I don't see much if any common ground that would lead to the development of a true agenda. POTUS, you were elected on the theme of, "Making America Great, Again!" I have seen progress as to Education Reforms and I hope that Congress follows suit, but let's not make it a Republican Issue!

There are issues that do not, repeat, do not need a political label, Education is one. Education is truly, an issue of State's Rights. Federal overreach should and must be re-defined as in an oversite service from Washington. This oversite should come in the form of standards in which the States can implement. Funding for each state would be part of the Department of Education's operation. Funding as including a voucher system should be a balance between public, charter, and voucher.

One way is not Senate Bill3 (SB-3), in my opinion had major issues. What we need is an education plan that is a true comprehensive set of reforms that will be a challenge to not just educators, but students as well!

Why is hard to understand that if one student slips through the cracks and fails, much less drops out, that's one too many. We need teacher's that are allowed to not just teach, but motivate students to learn!

The repeal of Obamacare, should never have been an issue of Partisan –politics. If memory is correct polls indicated that the people did not want the Affordable Care Act, despite its passage and Signing into law by Mr. Obama.

That media show at the White House was over doing it, quite a bit!

The missile attack on the Syrian military base made a lot of sense as in a sending a message to North Korea. Grant it, visiting with the representative of the Chinese government was also a good touch. Yet, that's not politics, that's Hollywood!

What our leadership needs, in both Austin and Washington is to lead. Find Common Ground, Period! Do not treat this as partisan politics. We are a nation of the people and expect the same in our government!

Journey XX

<u>A History, yet to be written...</u>

Recently I was reminded that our Constitution, stated that we specific rights, like "Freedom of Speech," to voice our opinions and thoughts. To that I offer this adventure as a foundation to open discussion, debate on a set of ideas to explore to make a new difference in America.

As a government, whether state or federal, are a government,"...of the People, By the People, and For the People," this journey began. I looked back at this project and realized that this book is one for discussion, debate, and down the road lead to true bipartisan change!

What we see in Government, today is anything, but bipartisanship. We see government in turmoil, a government angry and reacting to the public's outcry in a very heavy handed partisan manner.

What we as a people, need is a government that will remember that they serve the people.

I look out and see this every day in the eyes of American's who are angry, at a government who does not lead, but serves the politics that makes this one time honored profession,

"DIRTY!"

I look out and see American's are tired of the political infighting across the political aisles, both at State and Federal Levels. We have issues in Texas and the rest of the country that are best served in a bipartisan, rather than partisan politics.

Today, in Texas funding for Public Education is a hot topic issue, the problem in my opinion, is partisan politics is being played and no movement toward a workable solution, as in laying a stronger foundation on the horizon.

I feel that a bigger issue is when one student falls through the cracks and simply doesn't want to learn or eventually drops out of school.

I expanded my thoughts on Public Education to include my thoughts on Adult Literacy in Texas. While this is not a topic for partisan politics I offered this thought, as a means of helping those who can't read a means of motivation to want to learn. Social Media is such a vast experience, maybe Adult Literacy can place a link for themselves. I offered the idea of tax break and/or cuts to cellphone companies who donate smartphone, with literacy applications frontloaded on them, and air/data time reduced to that of a sliding scale, based upon ability to pay, this should help as a means of someone wanting to learn to read and cope.

I have offered a thought or two on our border with Mexico. A Wall along the border is not a solution, period! The answer could lies in a multi-step approach, (one plan included in this book, ror) supporting small businesses in South Texas, who employ Foreign Nationals, by offering tax breaks for said employees to become citizens.

This book, I offer as a means of opening the discussion, the debate. A means of moving forward and Making a New Difference!

With respect to the People,

Robb O. Rourke

Journey XXI
A Few Added Thoughts....

Since I officially finished this Journey, I found myself looking to take up another and voice my opinion once again. So, over the next few pages I will offer for your thoughts and opinions the following....

Well, I ended a long shift at Kroger's and I wanted to give a huge shout out to my co-workers, friends, and family as we gave our support of the Community. In a time that we see hardship, as a group, as a company strive to serve our community.

My biggest question, with all of the chaos around us, is can we do more to support the community?

We can pray for guidance. We can offer hand to those who have fallen, and a shoulder for them to lean on.

As a team we have advocated for helping students in need of school supplies. We have worked to feed the needy. We did it without earning a big salary. We did it because we care about our community.

Today, we helped our community in the aftermath of Harvey. And as we transition from a storm mode to that of clean up, we as a community must also look to the upcoming the upcoming school year.

We can look back to the most recent special session in Austin and wonder what in the,"________ ," are you thinking? Why is it so difficult to properly fund education in Texas, so our next generations can learn and build for future generations?

In writing this piece I read many of the postings as to the opinions of Austin, on facebook, and their lack of an opinion as to the community of Education in Texas.

So, we as a community, who care about the education of our children must come together; seek ideas and those who are willing to carry our message back to Austin in 2018 and 2020 to seek a proper education for our children.

To The State Legislature, All I say way to go.(Please note a sense of sarcasam, here! Ror) Education was underfunded, "AGAIN!" There is a bigger picture and yet I wonder if you all really do not understand our community of people and that the Education of each generation, past present and future needs to be maintained and properly funded, period!

Journey XXII
Epilogue and Thoughts of Others...

*These
are the ideas of a neo-populist whose time has come.*

Virginia C. Ward.

This is essential Robb Rourke. He is neither a knee jerk Liberal, or staunch conservative. His ideas and opinions reach out to both sides of the political aisle.

Michael D. Lane, former Chairman, 8th U.S. Congressional District, Commonwealth of Virginia.

In my opinion this is a good read for either side of the political aisle.

Darryl Eaton.

Journey XXIV
Gallery of Influence

My Mum...

To Boldly Go...

"We finally meet, Mr. Bond..."

Franklin Delano Roosevelt

Care packages for Troops abroad.

Family Portrait/Campaign 2004

My lone experience with the Republican Party in Virginia.

Backpack Boosters, 2017

Pride and Joy,
LOVE ALWAYS,
ShortCake

Visit with Santa,

With Kid Brother, many years ago....

In a Galaxy, far far away,

I had Hair. (Ha, Ha)

Junior Year 1976

Galveston Ball High

Selfie Attempt,

Not too bad, huh?

Journey XXV
<u>About the Author</u>

Well, I was born in a log cabin, along the Texas coast. (LOL)

A small joke.

I have always believed in America, and what it means to be American. What angers me is our government and their partisan approach legislating this country.

The Constitution say that we have the right to freedom of speech, and in this book I voice my opinions.

I grew up part of a Democratic family and looked into other opinions as to public policy. I spent time in the Republican Party of Virginia. Upon my return to Texas, I had an encounter with the Libertarian Party and found that my political home was with the Democrats of Texas.

One must realize that being from Texas, legends were born, and nurtured, based upon both fact and fiction.

Example; legend has it the Sam Houston challenged his troops to remember that 185 of their friends, neighbors and fellow Texans were holed up in a decaying mission buying them time,

And to this day we still,

"REMEMBER, THE ALAMO!"

The idea behind this adventure was to offer a framework of discussion as to answers to hot topics that affect our lives.

Education, as a whole we want our children to get a proper education, which means less government oversite, and more responsibility for the states. In Texas, it means more teachers, with good salaries, smaller class rooms, and a curriculum that will challenge and motivate students to learn.

Immigration, as a whole means security of our borders, especially with Mexico, but that does not means building a wall, whether the Government of Mexico pays for it or not! In Texas, it means supporting laws already in place. It means supporting ideas that for example are designed to support small businesses, along the southern border that have a population of employees who have a foreign origin, by tax breaks to employers that encourage said employees to become U.S. citizens.

Jobs, it means establishing a process for which those who are looking for a second career, to consider teaching as a second profession.

Technology, it means helping those who have issues with Adult Literacy.

This book is entitled

Journey to an Idea, making a new difference.

That difference will be defined by you the reader, as you seek a place to where it can be said that you had something to contribute. For me it has always been politics.

My father was a man that could best be described as always liked hearing himself talk. He talked about being Former President Lyndon B. Johnson's "Wingman in Texas," and when I found a political connection to a relative in New England, my father's comments, "We're one of the top political families in New England," and I had to ask, "We ended up in Texas, how?"

And the rest they say in Texas, are what legends are made of?

The Journey must Continue....